10/17

BIGGEST NAMES IN SPORTS

PATRICK KANE
HOCKEY STAR

by Marty Gitlin

FOCUS
READERS

WWW.NORTHSTAREDITIONS.COM

Produced for North Star Editions by Red Line Editorial.

Photographs ©: Nam Y. Huh/AP Images, cover, 1; Charles Rex Arbogast/AP Images, 4–5, 16–17; Mike Wulf/Cal Sport Media/AP Images, 7, 26; Shaun Best/Reuters/Alamy, 8–9; Jay LaPrete/AP Images, 11; Gene J. Puskar/AP Images, 12–13; Ryan Remiorz/Canadian Press/AP Images, 14; Brian Kersey/AP Images, 18; Matt Slocum/AP Images, 21; Chris O'Meara/AP Images, 22–23; Elise Amendola/AP Images, 25; Red Line Editorial, 29

ISBN
978-1-63517-042-9 (hardcover)
978-1-63517-098-6 (paperback)
978-1-63517-200-3 (ebook pdf)
978-1-63517-150-1 (hosted ebook)

Library of Congress Control Number: 2016951011

Printed in the United States of America
Mankato, MN
November, 2016

ABOUT THE AUTHOR

Marty Gitlin is a sportswriter and educational book author based in Cleveland, Ohio. He has had more than 100 books published, including dozens about famous athletes.

TABLE OF CONTENTS

CHAPTER 1

THE CLINCHER

The Chicago Blackhawks were close. They could almost taste their third National Hockey League (NHL) championship in six years.

It was June 15, 2015. The Blackhawks were playing the Tampa Bay Lightning in Game 6 of the **Stanley Cup** Final. They needed one more win to take the title.

Patrick Kane celebrates after scoring the clinching goal against the Lightning in Game 6 of the 2015 Stanley Cup Final.

They were clinging to a 1–0 lead with just over five minutes to play.

Chicago left wing Brandon Saad stole the puck. He bolted down the ice. Center Brad Richards and right wing Patrick Kane joined him on the attack.

Only two Lightning defenders could retreat in time. Saad passed the puck to Richards. Richards sent it to Kane. Kane fired a shot at the net. Tampa Bay goaltender Ben Bishop had no chance.

Soon the Blackhawks were hoisting the Stanley Cup. They had captured the title. And Kane had played the role of hero.

Kane had an **assist** on the first goal that night. He tied for the lead in playoff

Blackhawks captain Jonathan Toews (left) and Kane hold the Stanley Cup after winning it for the third time in six years.

points with 23. He finished second in goals with 11. Kane was simply amazing. But then, he had been simply amazing for years.

CHAPTER 2

LITTLE KID, BIG HEART

When he was growing up in Buffalo, New York, Patrick Kane was easy to spot on the ice. He was usually the smallest player in the game.

Patrick soon began standing out for other reasons, too. He was a fantastic player. He showed incredible stickhandling skills.

Kane (left) got used to being the smallest player on the ice a long time ago.

He easily broke free from defenders. He played with **passion**. He even got angry during neighborhood roller-hockey games when he thought his buddies were not playing with enough intensity.

Kane's father had been a high school hockey standout in Buffalo. He knew talent when he saw it. And when Patrick began outplaying older kids on the ice, his dad took notice. He drove his son to tryouts and clinics. Patrick played on travel teams. He bounced from one practice to the next. He often skated at three hockey rinks in the same day.

By age 11, Patrick was averaging nearly four points per game in local leagues.

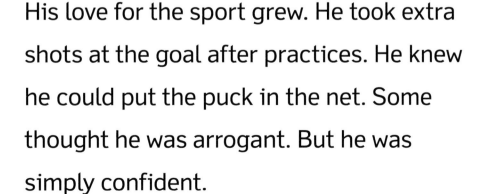

Kane (left) runs a drill with youth hockey players at a clinic held before the 2007 NHL draft.

His love for the sport grew. He took extra shots at the goal after practices. He knew he could put the puck in the net. Some thought he was arrogant. But he was simply confident.

CHAPTER 3

LEAVING HOME

Patrick Kane wanted to become the best hockey player he could be. That meant he needed stronger competition than he could find in Buffalo. When Patrick was 14 years old, an **elite** youth program had a spot available. But he had to move to Detroit, Michigan, to participate in the league.

Retired NHL star Pat Verbeek took Kane under his wing when the 14-year-old moved to Detroit.

Kane (left) stands with fellow NHL prospects Kyle Turris (center) and James van Riemsdyk before the 2007 draft.

Patrick left his family behind and moved in with a host family in Detroit. The father of that family was former NHL star Pat Verbeek. Verbeek had at least two things in common with Patrick. They both scored a lot of goals. And they were both small players.

Patrick led the US National Under-18 team in scoring in the 2005–06 season. The next year, he was named Ontario Hockey League (OHL) Rookie of the Year. He scored 145 points for the London Knights that season. And he was about to become an NHL star.

CHOOSING HIS OWN PATH

The coach with the most wins in NHL history gave Patrick advice in 2006. But Patrick didn't listen. Scotty Bowman suggested that Patrick play college hockey. But he chose to join the London Knights of the OHL instead. Patrick believed that playing in the OHL would put him on a faster path to the NHL.

CHAPTER 4

TURNING IT AROUND

The Chicago Blackhawks were terrible during the 2006–07 season. And they had been terrible the year before. In fact, they had been awful for a decade.

But bad teams have an advantage. They get high **draft** picks. The Blackhawks owned the first selection in the 2007 NHL draft. They used it on Patrick Kane.

Kane appears to like the fit of his Blackhawks sweater as he's introduced to the Chicago media on June 25, 2007.

Kane celebrates a goal during his rookie season.

A rookie is a first-year player. Rookies usually don't play a lot. But Kane was too talented to keep on the bench. He led the team in scoring with 21 goals and 51 assists. The Blackhawks even came close to making the playoffs. It was no surprise when Kane won the Calder Trophy as the NHL Rookie of the Year.

The Blackhawks had finally turned in the right direction. Kane led them to the playoffs in 2009. His **hat trick** in Game 6 of the second round clinched a win over the Vancouver Canucks. Kane flipped a backhand shot past goaltender Roberto Luongo to put the Canucks away. The fans at Chicago's United Center went crazy. They tossed hats onto the ice to celebrate Kane's first career hat trick.

A year later, the Blackhawks went all the way. Again, Kane was the hero. He led the Blackhawks into the Stanley Cup Final for the first time in 18 years.

In Game 6 against the Philadelphia Flyers, Kane scored a goal in **overtime** to give Chicago its first NHL title since 1961.

He did it with an amazing shot. Kane flipped the puck past Philadelphia goaltender Michael Leighton from the side of the net. The angle of the shot was

U-S-A! U-S-A!

Kane played for the US team in the 2010 and 2014 Winter Olympics. He scored three goals and two assists to help the Americans win a silver medal in 2010. He added four assists in six games in 2014. He also helped the US Men's National Under-18 team win a gold medal in 2006.

Kane celebrates with Blackhawks coach Joel Quenneville after winning the 2010 Stanley Cup Final.

so incredible that the TV announcers were not even aware Kane had scored.

But the Blackhawks knew. They poured onto the ice to celebrate. Kane had transformed his team from doormats to champions. And being champions would become a familiar feeling.

CHAPTER 5

TWO MORE TITLES

Fans in other NHL cities began packing arenas to watch Patrick Kane play. They wanted their teams to beat the Blackhawks. But they were in awe of Kane's talent. They marveled at his strong shots and quick moves. Even Kane's opponents appreciated the chance to see him in action.

Kane is a magician with the puck.

But Kane excited his Chicago teammates and fans more than anyone. He rose to the occasion when it mattered most. He was at his best in the playoffs.

In the 2013 Stanley Cup Final, Kane scored two goals in a Game 5 victory over the Boston Bruins. The Blackhawks won the championship that year. Kane was awarded the Conn Smythe Trophy. That honor is presented to the Most Valuable Player of the postseason. Kane had scored seven goals in the Blackhawks' final eight playoff games.

He has also amazed fans off the ice. In 2015, Kane responded to a request from a Chicago firefighter's wife. The couple

Kane admires the Conn Smythe Trophy after he won it during the 2013 Stanley Cup Playoffs.

had gone through tough times raising two special-needs children. Kane surprised the couple with a visit to the fire station.

Injuries soon slowed Kane. He sat out seven weeks of the 2014–15 season recovering from a broken collarbone.

Blackhawks fans can look forward to watching Kane (left) and Toews skate together for years.

But he recovered in time for the playoffs. He tallied two goals and five assists in a first-round defeat of the Nashville Predators. He scored five goals in a four-game sweep of the Minnesota Wild. He lifted Chicago into the Stanley Cup

Final with a three-assist game against the Anaheim Ducks. And he finished the job with his heroics against Tampa Bay.

The Blackhawks had been one of the worst teams in the NHL. But with Kane, they won three Stanley Cups in six years. The short player with big talent had turned the team around.

STICKING TOGETHER

The Blackhawks gave their fans a gift in July 2014. They announced that Kane and superstar teammate Jonathan Toews would be with the team for a long time. The team signed both to eight-year contract extensions. The deals were each worth more than $10 million per season.

PATRICK KANE

- Height: 5 feet 11 inches (180 cm)
- Weight: 177 pounds (80 kg)
- Position: Right wing
- Birth date: November 19, 1988
- Birthplace: Buffalo, New York
- Junior team: London Knights (2006–07)
- NHL team: Chicago Blackhawks (2007–)
- Major awards: Calder Trophy (2008);
    Conn Smythe Trophy (2013);
    Art Ross Trophy (2016)

London

Chicago

Buffalo

FOCUS ON
PATRICK KANE

Write your answers on a separate piece of paper.

1. Write a letter to a friend describing what you learned about Patrick Kane.

2. Do you think Patrick Kane made the right choice when he moved away from his family to play hockey as a teenager? Why or why not?

3. Which team did the Chicago Blackhawks defeat to win the Stanley Cup in 2015?
   - **A.** Minnesota Wild
   - **B.** Vancouver Canucks
   - **C.** Tampa Bay Lightning

4. Why was Patrick Kane named the NHL's Rookie of the Year in 2008?
   - **A.** The fans liked watching him play.
   - **B.** He was the best first-year player in the league.
   - **C.** He led Chicago to the playoffs.

Answer key on page 32.

GLOSSARY

assist
A pass or shot that leads directly to a teammate scoring a goal.

draft
A system that allows teams to acquire new players coming into a league.

elite
The best of the best.

hat trick
Three goals scored by one player in a game.

overtime
An extra period to determine a winner in a tie game.

passion
A strong feeling of love for a person or activity.

points
In hockey, goals and assists.

Stanley Cup
The NHL playoffs and the prize awarded to the champion.

TO LEARN MORE

BOOKS

Frederick, Shane. *Fantasy Hockey Math: Using Stats to Score Big in Your League.* Mankato, MN: Capstone Press, 2017.

Myers, Dan. *Hockey Trivia.* Minneapolis: Abdo Publishing, 2016.

Storden, Thom. *Amazing Hockey Records.* Mankato, MN: Capstone Press, 2015.

NOTE TO EDUCATORS

Visit **www.focusreaders.com** to find lesson plans, activities, links, and other resources related to this title.

INDEX

Answer Key: **1.** Answers will vary; **2.** Answers will vary; **3.** C; **4.** B